curious about

NINTENDO

BY RACHEL GRACK

A M I C U S

What are you

curious about?

CHAPTER THREE 3

Bet You Didn't Know ...

Curious About is published by Amicus
P.O. Box 227
Mankato, MN 56002
www.amicuspublishing.us

Editor: Alissa Thielges
Series and Book Designer: Kathleen Petelinsek
Cover Designer: Lori Bye
Photo Researcher: Omay Ayres

Library of Congress Cataloging-in-Publication Data
Names: Koestler-Grack, Rachel A., 1973– author.
Title: Curious about Nintendo / by Rachel Grack.
Description: Mankato, MN: Amicus, 2024. | Series: Curious about favorite brands | Includes bibliographical references and index. | Audience: Ages 5–9 | Audience: Grades 2–3 | Summary: "Nine kid-friendly questions give elementary readers an inside look at Nintendo to spark their curiosity about the brand's Japanese history, products, and cultural impact. A Stay Curious! feature models research skills while simple infographics support visual literacy"—Provided by publisher.
Identifiers: LCCN 2022032137 (print) | LCCN 2022032138 (ebook) | ISBN 9781645493297 (library binding) | ISBN 9781681528533 (paperback) | ISBN 9781645494171 (ebook)
Subjects: LCSH: Nintendo video games—History—Juvenile literature. | Video games industry—Juvenile literature.
Classification: LCC GV1469.32 .K66 2023 (print) | LCC GV1469.32 (ebook) | DDC 794.809—dc23/eng/20220708
LC record available at https://lccn.loc.gov/2022032137
LC ebook record available at https://lccn.loc.gov/2022032138

Photos © Alamy/ArcadeImages 9; INTERFOTO 7; Dreamstime/Artrosestudio 10–11; MarioWiki/marioparty 11 (Mario); Shutterstock/graphego 1, cover, m2art 22, 23 (controller), marysuperstudio 22, 23 (mushroom), Natsia27 15 (b), Nicescene 14, Sergei Bachlakov 18–19, Tinxi 16–17, Usa-Pyon 20–21, Vectorfair 11 (building); Wikimedia Commons/Eckhard Pecher 5 (t), Evan-Amos 12, 13, Haiko Honten Co. 4, Liane Enkelis 6, Marcus Richert 5 (b), Nintendo 8, Peer Schmidt 15 (t)

Printed in China

CHAPTER ONE

Who started Nintendo?

Nintendo's first main office (left) had a name plate (top right) outside.

It began in Japan in 1889. Wait . . . what? That was before video games! Yep. Fusajiro Yamauchi was an artist. He made beautiful cards for *Hanafuda*. This is a popular card game in Japan. He sold other games and toys, too. Nintendo quickly became Japan's top game company.

Hanafuda is still played today.

DID YOU KNOW?
***Hanafuda* means "flower card."**

When did Nintendo start making video games?

Ralph Baer was an inventor and engineer.

In the 1970s. In 1972, Ralph Baer invented the home video game **console**. He hooked an electronic ping-pong game up to a TV. It was called Odyssey. Nintendo bought the rights to sell the game in Japan. Before long, Nintendo came up with its own console. Today, it is one of the biggest video game **brands** in the world!

Odyssey looked like two people playing tennis.

CHAPTER TWO

What was Nintendo's first video game?

EVR Race in 1975. The **arcade** racing game did OK. Then *Donkey Kong* came out in 1981. This was a hit! It had a little man in a red cap. He could jump over rolling barrels. He was the first character to do that. The goal was to save his girlfriend from a wacky gorilla. Back then, that character was named Jumpman. You know him as Mario.

DID YOU KNOW?
***Super Mario Bros.* has sold more than 40 million copies. It is one of the best-selling video games of all time!**

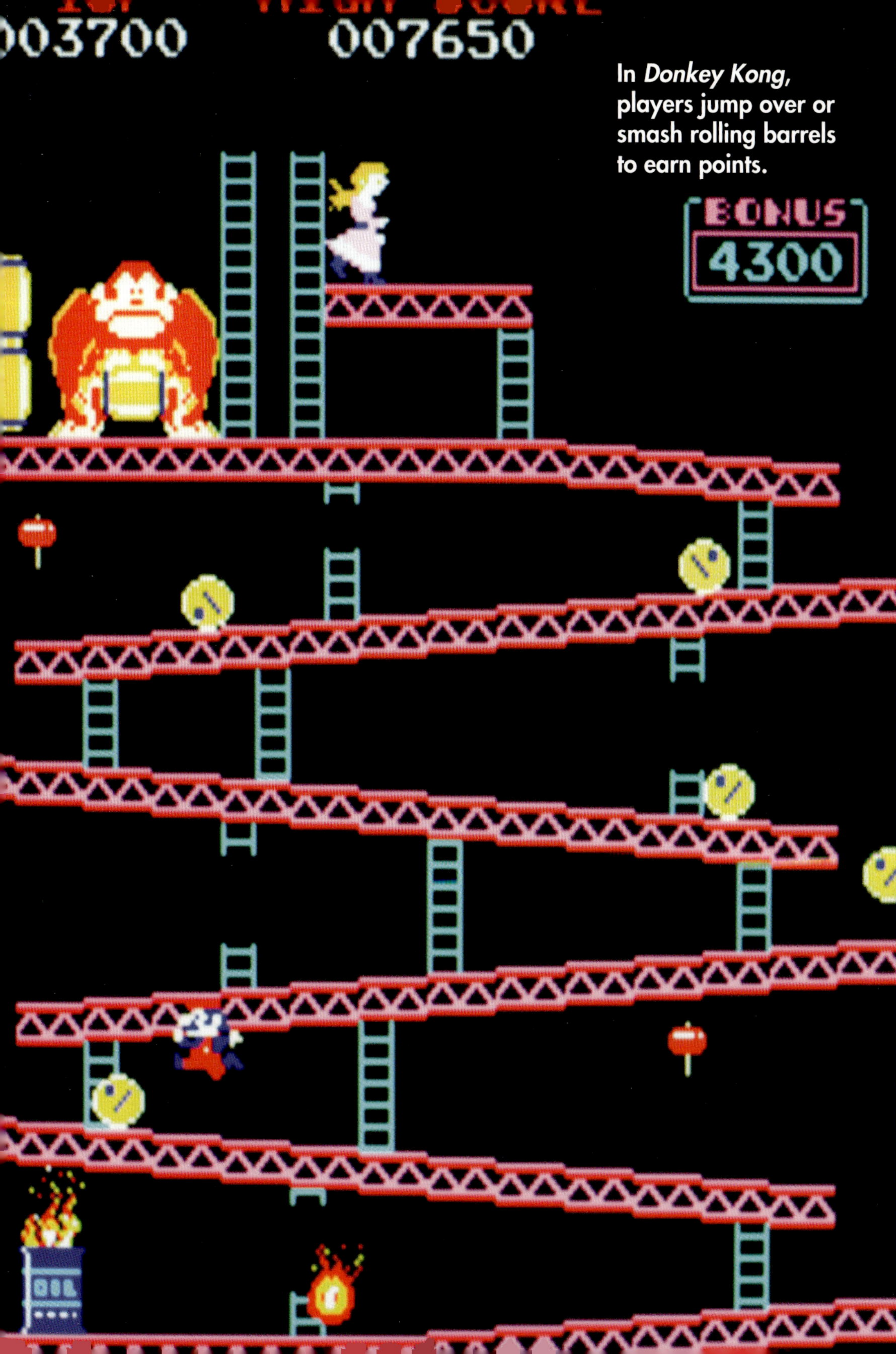

In *Donkey Kong*, players jump over or smash rolling barrels to earn points.

Why was Jumpman named Mario?

Mario explores an underground level in Super Mario Bros.

It happened at a Nintendo meeting. The team was trying to come up with a new name for Jumpman. At that moment, Mario Segale stormed into the room. He was the landlord of the office in America. He was bold and feisty. The team thought his name fit their character perfectly.

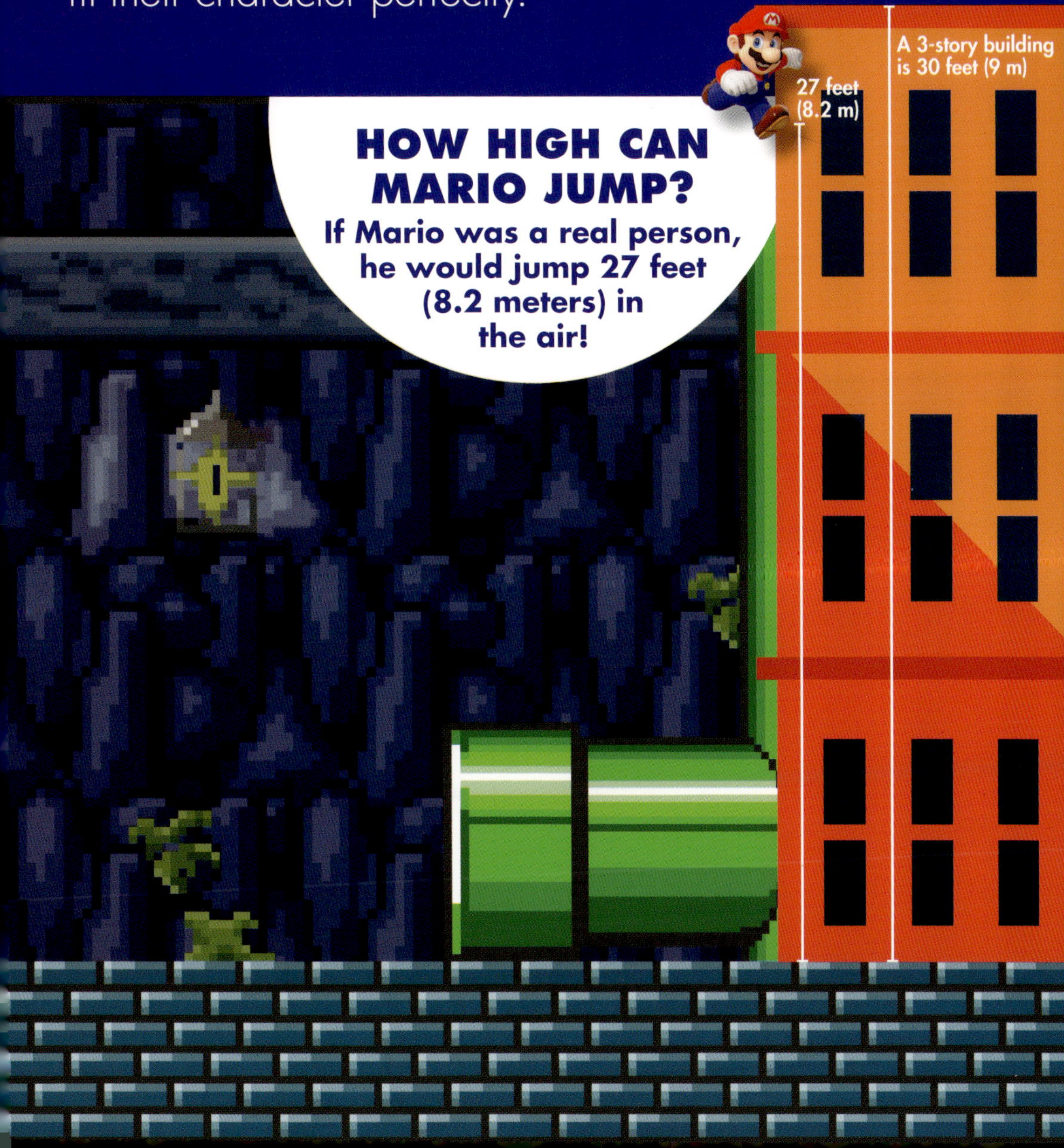

HOW HIGH CAN MARIO JUMP?

If Mario was a real person, he would jump 27 feet (8.2 meters) in the air!

What was Nintendo's first home gaming system?

Two people could play the Color TV-Game.

Color TV-Game led the way in 1977. But it only played one game. Nintendo Entertainment System (NES) soon followed. This console used changeable game **cartridges**. Nintendo has made 13 different home game consoles. The Wii was the first gaming system with **motion** controls. It quickly became a best seller!

MOST POPULAR NINTENDO GAMING SYSTEMS

NINTENDO DS
RELEASED 2004
OVER 154 MILLION SOLD

GAME BOY
RELEASED 1989
OVER 118 MILLION SOLD

NINTENDO SWITCH
RELEASED 2017
OVER 103 MILLION SOLD

NINTENDO Wii
RELEASED 2006
OVER 101 MILLION SOLD

GAME BOY ADVANCE
RELEASED 2001
OVER 81 MILLION SOLD

What was the first handheld game for Nintendo?

Game and Watch in 1980. It could fit in your pocket. The idea came from a calculator! It only played one game, though. Next came Game Boy in 1989. It was fun, easy to play, and had a long-lasting battery. Like NES, it used cartridges. Today, Nintendo Switch is both a home and handheld console.

DID YOU KNOW?
Game Boy brought Pokémon to life for the first time. Nintendo and Pokémon have worked together ever since.

You can play the Switch at home or on the go.

CHAPTER THREE

Can I get paid to play video games when I grow up?

Testers play the same game over and over until it is perfect.

Yes! Nintendo hires professional game testers. These players try new games before they hit stores. But this job takes more than mad gaming skills. Testers look for **bugs** in games. They figure out how the bugs happen. Then, they make sure the problems get fixed.

Could I win a Nintendo gaming contest?

Some cities have local video game contests.

Maybe. Be sure to practice first. Kids can play Nintendo games in online **tournaments**. These cost money, though. So, check with an adult before signing up. There is even a Nintendo Switch tournament for classrooms! Nintendo wants to get kids excited about computer jobs.

Are there Nintendo parks?

Yes. In 2021, the first Super Nintendo World opened in Japan. Another is at Universal Studios Hollywood in California. The **theme parks** have Nintendo rides, games, and shops. Meet Mario, Luigi, and Princess Peach in Mushroom Kingdom.

The parks look like life-sized video games.

ASK MORE QUESTIONS

How many Nintendo systems are there?

What are the latest Nintendo games?

Try a BIG QUESTION: What would it take to make my own video game?

SEARCH FOR ANSWERS

Search the library catalog or the Internet.
A librarian, teacher, or parent can help you.

Using Keywords
Find the looking glass.

Keywords are the most important words in your question.

If you want to know about:

- Nintendo systems, type: NINTENDO GAMING SYSTEMS
- the latest games, type: NEW NINTENDO GAMES

LEARN MORE

FIND GOOD SOURCES

Are the sources reliable?
Some sources are better than others. An adult can help you. Here are some good, safe sources.

Books

Super Mario
by Mari Bolte, 2022.

What Is Nintendo?
by Gina Shaw, 2020.

Internet Sites

Play Nintendo!
https://play.nintendo.com/
Play Nintendo is an interactive website for kids with Nintendo games, videos, and information.

TED-ed: A Brief History of Video Games
https://ed.ted.com/lessons/a-brief-history-of-video-games-part-i-safwat-saleem
TED-ed is a non-profit educational site with videos on many topics.

Every effort has been made to ensure that these websites are appropriate for children. However, because of the nature of the Internet, it is impossible to guarantee that these sites will remain active indefinitely or that their contents will not be altered.

SHARE AND TAKE ACTION

Think up an idea for a new video game.
Ask your friends to help. Draw out your ideas. Come up with a catchy name.

Talk to a computer programmer who makes video games.
Maybe you can learn some new gaming skills!

Have a gaming tournament!
Pick your favorite Nintendo game. Compete with friends, alone, or on teams.

GLOSSARY

arcade A place where people play coin-operated video games.

brand A group of products made or owned by the same company.

bug In games, a problem that prevents a program or system from working properly.

cartridge A plastic case that holds a computer program that is inserted into a gaming system.

console A gaming unit that hooks up to a TV for play.

motion The act of moving.

theme park A large park with rides, activities, restaurants, and buildings that are all based around certain characters or fictional worlds.

tournament A contest that includes many players or teams and is usually several days long.

INDEX

About the Author

Rachel Grack has been editing and writing children's books since 1999. She lives on a small ranch in southern Arizona. She enjoys watching her grandchildren play the original Pokémon games on her Nintendo 64 console.